MW00851217

I suppose children have always needed clear, biblical guidance on sex and sexuality, but it also seems that today's challenges – abundant and accessible pornography, new societal norms regarding gender, the widespread celebration of homosexuality, and so much more – require parents to be especially proactive. I'm thankful for *Not If, But When* and its simple, appropriate, and Bible-based lessons on the purpose and the power, the blessings and the boundaries, of God's gift of sexuality.

Tim Challies
Blogger at www.challies.com

How did you learn about sex? For all the wonderful things my parents did for me, I never had 'the talk' with either of them. I cobbled together ideas from friends, TV, books, and pornography I had seen as an adolescent. When I speak on sexuality and relationships around the country, I often ask the audience to raise their hands if, as youth, they had a helpful, ongoing discipleship conversation regarding sexuality with a parent or mentor. The answer is pretty much the same: about 5% or less! *Not If, But When* is an excellent resource to change that percentage in the right direction. With biblical clarity, gentleness and easy-to-follow examples, John Perritt's new book will help parents and caregivers grow in wisdom and courage to disciple children in sexual faithfulness.

Ellen Mary Dykas
Women's Ministry Coordinator for Harvest USA
Author *Sexual Sanity for Women: Healing from Sexual and Relational Brokenness*,

It's a hard thing to admit or even to think about – but we live in a sexualised society where pornography is the norm. We want to protect our children but to ignore what is happening in the wider culture will not protect. Rather, our children need to be taught openly and in a culturally appropriate way what the Bible teaches. *Not If, But When* does just that. An excellent resource for parents to use.

David Robertson
Well-known Pastor and Apologist

Dedication

To some of God's greatest treasures in my life – Sarah, Samuel, Jillian, Will, and Amber. Even though you are growing up in a world poisoned by sin, I pray you see the goodness and beauty of God's creation and grow to see him as your Creator, Redeemer, and Friend. I love you more than you love me!

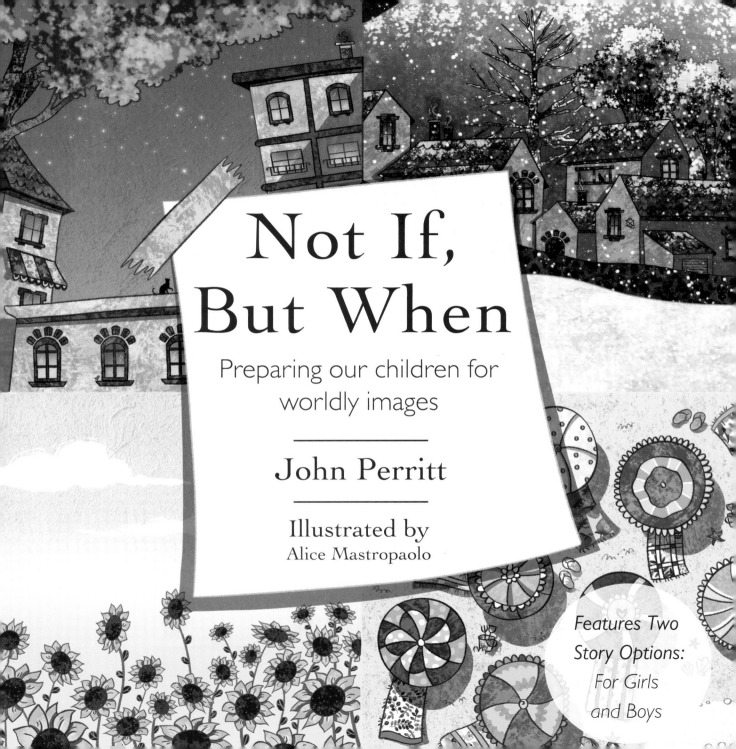

Not If, But When

Preparing our children for
worldly images

———————

John Perritt

———————

Illustrated by
Alice Mastropaolo

Features Two Story Options: For Girls and Boys

Contents

Introduction for Parents

When I decided to have "the talk" with my oldest child, I fixed a picnic lunch and, by God's grace, it turned out to be a truly beautiful moment between father and daughter. I read some portions of Genesis, explained God's glorious gift of sex and his creating male and female as sexual beings. I allowed her to ask questions which helped me steer the conversation in an age-appropriate way. While I'm sure some of my explanations were less than perfect, it seemed like a perfect time spent together and I was so thankful to God for that time I hope we'll both remember for many years to come. Little did I know, however, just how thankful I would be.

Two months after this conversation I was in the living room with my wife enjoying some quiet conversation as our children played in the front yard. Our yard often became the hangout for all the neighborhood children. I would typically step outside on occasion to ensure everyone was playing nice – trying to strike a balance between the helicopter parent and the neglectful parent. Before I could step outside my daughter and her friend came in. Just as I sensed that something was wrong, my daughter said, "Dad, can we talk to you?"

My daughter and her friend told me that two boys down the street asked them to have sex with them. My daughter and the two boys she referenced were eight-years-old and the other girl was about six … let that sink in. She went on to explain that they were saying some other sexual things – not her words – and they rode away on their bikes and came to talk to me.

Then my daughter said, "Part of me didn't want to tell you this, but I knew I should." I praised her for this decision and thanked God for moving in her heart to bring this information to me.

After I spoke with the girls, I tracked down the two boys. (Yes, they are both still alive today for those wondering.) God gave me firm but gracious words. One boy literally began to tear up and almost cried in front of me. It was that quivering lip and those glossy eyes that God used to give me this thought, It's not this boy's fault. It's his parents.

I could be mistaken, but I assume this young boy did not know what sex was. He has probably heard the word and – if we're going with statistics – seen pornographic images. But, hearing the word 'sex' in the school halls or seeing sexual images on Google are not sex.

God's definition of sex is far deeper than any image on the Internet. It's even beyond the understanding of any adult who's been married for fifty years. God's gift of sex is his glorious invention that's shared between one man and one woman in the context of marriage and it points to his love for his church.

We may know what sex is, but we will never fully know the great depth God created it to be. This is what makes pornography such a tragedy.

What took place in my front yard that day was tragic. Two young girls were hurt and scared. It's difficult for adults to comprehend the ways in which their young minds processed the sexual requests of these boys. But, it's not only a tragedy for these young girls, it also is for these boys. Even though I tried to communicate love and truth to them, I hardly have a relationship with them. I could only do so much. Without God's intervention, they will continue down a path of sexual perversion and hurt others in the process.

I hope I'm wrong and maybe they have parents that are teaching them about biblical sexuality. But, this book is written for them. It's written for the two little girls who came walking in my living room that day. It's written for parents who know that it's not a matter of *if my child will be exposed to pornography, but when will they be exposed.*

Pornography is wreaking havoc in our culture. After serving in youth ministry for well over a decade, I've seen students, families, and marriages destroyed over this issue. I've had parents and students in my office in tears over this issue. And I'm convinced that one of the greatest tools the enemy has used when it comes to pornography has been this: silence.

Too many parents have been embarrassed or felt ill-equipped to deal with this subject, so they don't talk about it at all. They remain silent on the matter.

Sadly, some of the silence from the parents has been due to the fact that they have secret porn addictions themselves. Other parents mistakenly think that remaining silent about it will protect their children from it. While there are numerous reasons parents don't talk about this issue, let's consider one way to fight against the pervasive influence of pornography in our culture.

As you've probably guessed, if silence has been a weapon pornography has employed, then conversation is an ally in our fight. But, I'm not simply talking about passing on a knowledge about pornography and its devastating effects, which can be helpful. I'm talking about passing on the truth of God's Word to our children. That's where this book comes in.

The book you hold in your hand is meant to be read alongside your child. It is pitched at 7–12-year-olds. While some of you may protest that seven is too young, please be reminded that the average age of porn exposure is now eight-years-old. Plus, wouldn't you want your children to be exposed to the truth of God's Word about sex before they hear lies from the world?

It is my hope and prayer that God uses this resource to protect many young minds from a life of pornography. That God uses this resource to spare future marriages the affliction brought from pornography. And, while we can be confident that God does use his Word to transform lives, we must be in prayer. This resource is not a guarantee that your life and the life of your children will be free of pornography abuse. That said, it is a mighty tool I hope the Lord is pleased to use in our fight against this issue.

Introduction
To be Read with Child

One of the greatest gifts God gives to parents are children – they are treasures! The truth is, however, our children don't belong to us but to God. Since God creates everything, it all belongs to him – even children. Therefore, part of a parent's job is to take care of the children God gifts to them.

One of the jobs I have as your parent is to take care of you. Not only do I try and take care of your physical needs – like food, shelter, and clothing, but, I also try and take care of your spiritual needs – like praying for you and reading the Bible with you. This little workbook is part of how I'm trying to faithfully parent you to be a godly person in a sinful world.

Something I want to teach you about is God's good gift of sex and how our sinful world affects it. In Genesis 1:26–28 we read:

> "Then God said, 'Let us make man in our image, after our likeness. And let them have dominion over the fish of the sea and over the birds of the heavens and over the livestock and over all the earth and over every creeping thing that creeps on the earth.' So God created man in his own image, in the image of God he created him; male and female he created them. And God blessed them. And God said to them, 'Be fruitful and multiply and fill the earth and subdue it, and have dominion over the fish of the sea and over the birds of the heavens and over every living thing that moves on the earth.'"

There is so much that could be said about these verses. One thing these verses discuss is God's design of sex. When God is telling Adam and Eve to be "fruitful and multiply and fill the earth …" he's talking about sex. To be sure, he's talking about more than sex, but he is telling Adam and Eve to do something he created them to do. They are to have sex and by doing this they will be fruitful, multiply, and fill the earth.

The most important thing I want you to hear from me is that God created sex and it is a good thing. He actually created it and it was a part of life before sin even entered the world.

Sadly, sin enters the world in chapter 3 of Genesis. After that, sin poisoned everything. The world is still good and contains God's amazing fingerprints all over it, but sin has also impacted every square inch – even sex.

What this workbook discusses is one specific way that sex has been poisoned by sin. There is something called "pornography" and it is just one way we see sin ruining something God created as good. Pornography is a dangerous thing and it hurts you and other people. Not only do I want to teach you about this to protect you, but I also want to teach you about this so you can understand God's good creation.

Even though I cannot protect you from all the evils of this world, I can pass the knowledge of God's Word on to you and equip you for life in a broken world. The Bible tells us that it is the Sword of the Spirit (Ephesians 6:17). God uses it in our lives as a weapon against evil. In order for me to be a faithful parent, I want to equip you with the truth of God's Word in the midst of a world that lies to you. Pornography is a lie that will hurt you, so let's read the truth of God's Word to fight it.

(For the boy's story, turn to page 35)

12

Not If, But When

The Girl's Story

1. One of God's Greatest Gifts

"How was the waterpark?" Nancy asked. Sarah and her friends had been anticipating this trip for the past month. Not only would it be a fun place to visit, but it marked the end of school as well.

"Oh Mom! It was such fun," Sarah replied. "Everyone was able to make it and the weather was perfect. Plus, there was no school."

Laughing, her mother said, "I'm glad you had fun, but remember, school isn't to punish children. It helps you steward the brain God has given you." This was a phrase that had become very familiar to Sarah.

"Hey Mom," Sarah said somberly. "You know how you said we can always talk to you about anything?"

"Of course you can sweetie," Nancy replied. Nancy sensed a concern in Sarah's tone.

"Well, my friends were talking about this boy at the waterpark. They said he looked cute and one of my friends said he had a good body. They also said something about sex."

Read:
Genesis 1:1, 26-28

Main Point:
God made all things, even something called sex.

What did you learn?
(Allow your child to answer in their own words.) God made all things and this includes sex. Sex is a good thing – a gift – God has given to his children.

"Thank you for telling me that," said Nancy. "Do you remember exactly what they said about sex?"

"Nothing much. They just used the word. I don't even think they knew what it meant."

"Honey, I'm so glad you're coming to me with this and not to someone else. You're showing a lot of wisdom to talk with someone older about something as important as sex. To be honest, I should have talked to you about this sooner, so please forgive Mommy for not doing that. Do you remember how the Bible begins?"

"Yes," said Sarah, "it tells us that God made all things. And that he created men and women 'after his own image'."

"That's right," said Nancy, "and, if you remember, God also tells humans to be 'fruitful and multiply' and 'to fill the earth'. What do you think God's talking about there?"

Sarah, looking down at the floor, replied, "Is God telling them to make babies?"

Nancy said, "That's part of what he's telling them. You see, when we read Genesis we read that God made everything. But, it doesn't specifically say that God created sex. Even though it doesn't use the word 'sex' in Genesis, that is some of what is meant by 'fill the earth and multiply'. God wants men and women to have sex in the proper context."

Thinking a bit about what her mother said, "So sex is how babies are made?"

"That's right," said Nancy. "You know how Mommy and Daddy tell you that you are an amazing gift to us? Well, sex is also an amazing gift. God made it and gave it to us and it is just one of the ways that tells us what a gracious and loving God we have."

Sarah replied, "So, when sex is a good thing, why did I feel like we were talking about something bad at the waterpark?"

"That's a great question, sweetie. Let's go on the back deck and talk about this some more."

2. The Gift's Instructions

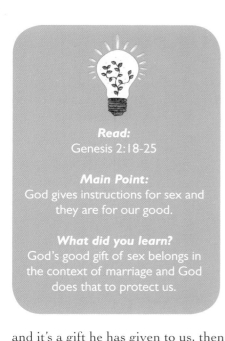

Read:
Genesis 2:18-25

Main Point:
God gives instructions for sex and they are for our good.

What did you learn?
God's good gift of sex belongs in the context of marriage and God does that to protect us.

As Nancy poured a glass of lemonade, Sarah finished hers in one gulp. "Slow down and enjoy it."

"I'm just so thirsty, Mom. It was so hot at the waterpark."

"Sarah, you asked an insightful question about sex. You felt a little guilty when you talked about it? Well, there's a few reasons why you probably felt that way. The first thing you should know about sex is that it is a very intimate action between a husband and wife. When you read the end of Genesis 2 it says, 'the man and his wife were both naked and were not ashamed.' They were not ashamed because sin had not entered the earth. There was no shame in the man and woman being naked because it was just the two of them. I know they were the only two people on the earth, but you need to know that sex is a private and intimate thing. Something that's just supposed to be shared between a husband and wife. In other words, it's not something your friends should be talking about at the waterpark. Especially since they probably don't even know what it means."

"That makes sense," said Sarah. "But, Mom, if it's a good thing God made and it's a gift he has given to us, then why is it so secret and why did I feel guilty?"

Pouring another glass of lemonade, Nancy said, "Well, since God created sex, he also gives us instructions on how humans should enjoy this good gift. And, just like the gift God gives, the instructions are good too. They are there to protect us. And, two important instructions have to do with context and timing."

"Context and timing?" Sarah questioned. "What exactly do you mean?"

Thinking intently, Nancy said, "Sarah, do you remember that time you got in trouble with Mrs. Smith?"

Feeling a sense of shame, Sarah said, "Yes."

Nancy quickly replied, "Sweetie, I'm not trying to make you feel guilty. We talked about that situation and you are forgiven. I just thought of a way to explain context to you. You see, Mrs. Smith punished you and your friends because you were talking in class. But, let me ask you this, is talking with your friends a bad thing?"

A bit unsure, Sarah replied, "No?"

"Well," said Nancy, "you could also say 'yes.' That is, there are times you can talk to your friends and times you can't. Talking while the teacher is speaking is one time when you can't. To say it another way, there are certain contexts when you can talk with your friends and certain contexts when you can't."

"That makes sense," said Sarah. "So, there are times when you can have sex and times when you can't."

"Exactly!" said Nancy. "The Bible tells us that sex is only okay in the context of marriage. Whenever you take God's good gift of sex out of his good instructions on context, it actually ends up hurting us. Does that make sense?"

Nodding, Sarah replied, "Yes, I understand. That's why I felt a little guilty talking about it with my friends."

Nancy nodded, "Now, let me explain what I mean by timing …"

3. Opening the Gift too Early

Read:
Song of Solomon 2:7, 3:5, 8:4

Main Point:
Marriage is the context for sex, so we must be cautious of stirring up sexual desires too soon.

What did you learn?
God gives each of us sexual desires, but we must be cautious of stirring those emotions up too soon.

Nancy's focus was diverted to the sound of the backdoor swinging open as she saw her son, Samuel, come sprinting toward her. After giving his mother a hug, Samuel said, "Mom, that was such a cool movie. Thanks for letting me go over to Carl's house."

"You're welcome. So glad you had fun. Listen," said Nancy. "I'm having a talk with Sarah about something you cannot hear about. One day I'll talk to you about it, but not today. Would you please go inside and play with Dad while we talk?"

Samuel hardly let his mom finish as he began running inside. "Sure thing, Mom!" he called out as the door slammed closed.

Sarah and Nancy both smiled at each other and returned to their talk about sex. "So, marriage is the context for sex." Sarah said. "You were about to say something about timing?"

"That's right," said Nancy. "There's a verse in the biblical book called the Song of Solomon. It's a book about love and marriage. One of the verses that's repeated many times is this, 'Do not stir up or awaken love until it pleases.' This basically means that there's an appropriate time for sex."

Sarah reclined in her seat as she listened to her mother. "You see, since God created man and woman for sex, we are sexual beings. What that means is we all have sexual desires in us. Your friends, for example, at the waterpark were expressing some sexual desires when they saw that boy they thought was cute. How would you apply the verse from Song of Solomon to this situation with your friends?"

A bit surprised by her mother's question, Sarah said, "Uh … I guess … it would mean that we should be careful talking about cute boys? I mean, we could be stirring up desires too soon."

"That's a really thoughtful answer, sweetie. You are right, you have to be careful talking about sex and love because they are strong desires that God has created. And, he has created them to bind two people together in a deep way. Therefore, if you talk about sexual desires too often, you might 'awaken love' in a way that's removing it from its proper context."

"Mom, if talking about sexual desires might awaken love too soon, is it bad for us to be talking about it? I mean, I'm thinking about it right now, so is this a bad thing?"

"That's such a smart question," said Nancy. "As your mother, it's part of my job to tell you about sex and love. Remember, God has created you as a sexual being, so you're going to have sexual desires regardless of whether or not your father and I talk about it. You see, we need to have these talks, so you know what to do when you have these desires. You don't need to feel guilty for having these desires, because God gave them to you. One thing you need to do when you feel those desires is talk to me or Daddy and, most importantly, talk to God about them in prayer."

4. Distorting the Gift

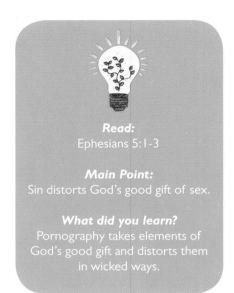

Read:
Ephesians 5:1-3

Main Point:
Sin distorts God's good gift of sex.

What did you learn?
Pornography takes elements of God's good gift and distorts them in wicked ways.

"Hey Mom." As those words came out of Sarah's mouth, Nancy sensed a tone of guilt. "Something else happened at the waterpark. When we were finishing up for the day, Stephanie showed me some pictures on her phone. Some of them were guys with their shirts off, but some of them showed guys naked."

"Oh sweetie. I am so sorry you saw that."

"You told me I could talk to you about anything, so I wanted to tell you about this."

Nancy moved over toward Sarah and put her arm around her. "I'm so happy you told me about this. You did the right thing. Sarah, those pictures are something we call pornography. Pornography is pictures of people that are either naked or barely clothed."

"Mom, I knew I shouldn't be looking at them and I didn't look at them long, but I was caught off guard when Stephanie showed them to me. I felt like it would be weird if I didn't look or if I asked her to stop showing them to me. I didn't know what to do, so I just acted like I liked them."

"I completely understand," said Nancy. "This is part of why it is so important for us to talk about sex. Sadly, we live in a sinful world and humans have taken God's good gift of sex and distorted it in many ways. Pornography is just one way sinful humans distort the gift of sex."

"Mom, why are my friends looking at pornography?"

Nancy paused to think a minute before she responded. "Well, if you think about what we've discussed, it makes sense. God created all of us to be sexual creatures, but in the proper context. Pornography steals parts of God's gift and uses it in inappropriate and evil ways. All of that to say, your friends are enticed by pornography – in part – because they're created as sexual beings. Does that make sense?"

"I think it does," Sarah said.

Nancy explained some more, "Even though pornography is taking sexual desires out of their context, it still contains aspects of God's good gift of sex."

"I get it now," Sarah smiled.

"That's what makes pornography so dangerous. It is using elements of God's gift, but it's twisting them in horrible ways. This is what Paul meant when he talked about sexual immorality. There are a lot of things that could be described as sexual immorality, pornography is one of them."

5. Worshiping the Gift

Read:
Genesis 1:26-28

Main Point:
God gives value to humans
by creating them in his image,
pornography devalues humans by
objectifying them.

What did you learn?
Pornography attempts to
turn people into objects and
disrespects them. God created
people as his image-bearers and
gives them value because of that.

Sarah crumpled up another tissue and threw it into the garbage can. Talking about some of the images she saw on Stephanie's phone really upset her, so Nancy had brought her into their study to console her in privacy.

Nancy, curling Sarah's hair between her fingers, said, "Sweetie, I know this was such an upsetting thing for you and I'm so sorry you had to see those pictures. Part of the reason you are so upset is because of how God created us as humans. You see, he has created everyone – male and female, young and old, black or white – after his own image. Therefore, every human reflects his glory and deserves respect. Pornography, however, disrespects people."

"Mom, I know pornography is wrong as it removes sex out of the right context you talked about, but how does it disrespect people?"

"Well, lets think," said Nancy. "I don't want to upset you, but I want to ask you a question about the picture you saw. Did you see the man's face?"

"It didn't show his face, Mom."

"That's what I thought. Often pornography doesn't focus on the faces of the men or women in the pictures. Sometimes it does, but sometimes it doesn't. What pornography does is focus on body parts. It's trying to just give us pictures of the sexual parts of people, without us seeing the person. The word for this is 'objectifying.' Pornography tells us to focus on people as objects to use how we want, instead of as people. This is against the way God created us."

"I understand. God made all of us to reflect his image," said Sarah, "but pornography tries to get us to focus on different parts of people, which … objectifies them and disrespects them?"

"That's right. Once again, it's taking sex out of the context God created it for. It's taking sex out of the context of marriage and tries to give it to people in a way that's inappropriate. Pornography tricks people into thinking they can take God's gift and use it in another way, but they only end up hurting themselves when they do that. Remember, sex was created to bind a man and a woman together in a loving way. Pornography removes the loving relationship of our sexuality and focuses on sexual parts."

"Now that I think about it," said Sarah, "all the other girls were talking about the guy in the picture and they were just talking about his body. They weren't talking about him like a person."

"Yes, and this goes against the way God created humans. Again, people are God's image-bearers and that means they deserve respect, but pornography attempts to take that away from people. Pornography disrespects people."

"I see. I felt bad after seeing those pictures and I see how pornography disrespects people … but, why did my friends enjoy it?"

"That's an important question," said Nancy.

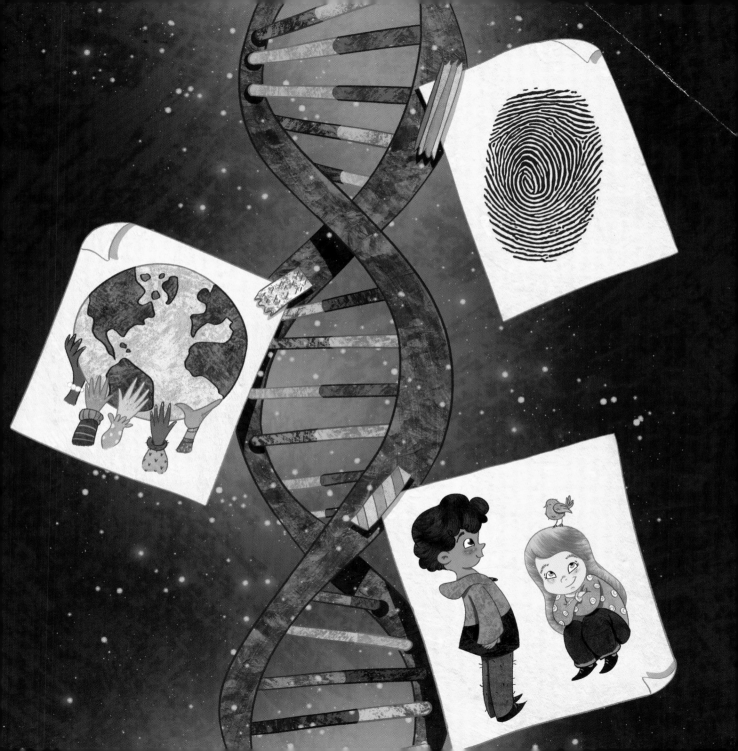

6. Enjoying the Gift

Read:
Matthew 5:27-30

Main Point:
God gives humans sexual desires, but sin often turns that into lust.

What did you learn?
God gives all of us sexual desires that are good. Because of our sin, those desires are affected and we can sin against God by lusting.

"As I told you earlier," Nancy said, "God created every person with sexual desires[1]. But, every human on the face of the earth is also a sinner; therefore, these sexual desires can get confused. To say it another way, the good sexual desires God gave us can also become sinful."

"So, my friends were looking at those pictures, because God created them as sexual people?"

"That's right."

"But, they were in sin, because they weren't using the desires in a way God created them to?"

"Exactly!" said Nancy. "We describe sexual sin as lust. Lust is a word that can refer to more than our sexuality, but it means a really strong desire for something you cannot have. When Jesus was speaking in the Sermon on the Mount, he warned us about lust. You see, many people in his day thought they were obeying the Ten Commandments because they didn't literally commit adultery with another person's spouse. But, Jesus teaches that if you even lust after someone in your heart you are committing adultery with them in your mind."

"Were my friends lusting when they looked at those pictures?"

"Most likely they were."

"Was I lusting, Mom?"

"Well, it sounds like you were pretty upset because you were caught off guard by these images. You also were not seeking them out, so in a sense, you weren't lusting after these images. That said, the images were sinful and inappropriate for you to look at. The important thing is that you told me about these and now we're able to have this talk."

"Yes Ma'am."

"Sweetie. You don't need to feel bad that you will have sexual desires in your life. Remember, God created you to have sexual attraction. Does that make sense?" Sarah nodded in agreement.

"The important truth is that you ask the Holy Spirit to help you with those desires. When Jesus taught about lusting, he was telling everyone how badly they need him. When he spoke on lusting, he was telling everyone that they sin sexually and need him to cleanse them. Sarah, you will not be able to live a perfect life, especially when it comes to sex, but ask God to give you strength to honor him with your sexuality. Let's pray and ask God for that now."

1. See Endnotes

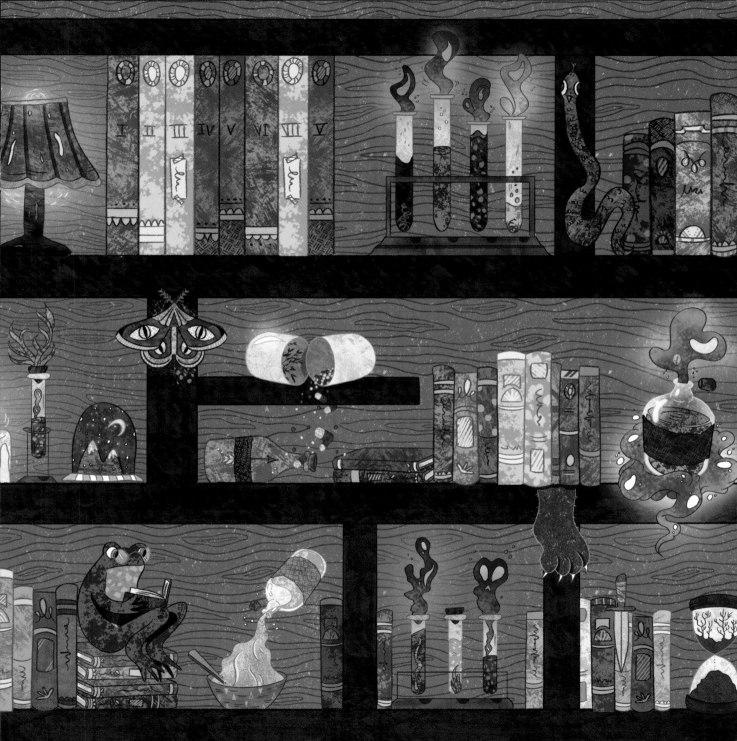

7. Breaking the Gift

As Sarah looked around the room, her mother could tell she was processing the conversation. Instead of speaking, Nancy just sat in silence to let Sarah think.

Sarah finally broke the silence and said, "I know I've got a question; but let me think back through all you've said." Nancy smiled and nodded.

"God created men and women and invented sex as a good thing," said Sarah. Nancy nodded in affirmation. "He made us as sexual beings in his image, but we sinned against him."

Nodding again, Nancy said, "That's correct."

"Pornography is a result of our sin and it objectifies people and causes us to lust … which is like adultery."

"All of that is correct, sweetie."

"Are there other ways that pornography hurts people?"

"Yes, there are," Nancy replied. "Actually, there are many, many ways it hurts people."

The discussion was interrupted with a knock at the door. Nancy's husband, Ron, entered the room and could tell the two were engaged in a serious discussion. "Need me to help with dinner tonight?"

"That would be great, Ron. Sarah and I are talking about issues surrounding sex."

"I'd be happy to be a part of the discussion if you'd like?"

"That would be great. Maybe we can all talk about it a bit later," Nancy replied.

"Okay, just let me know how I can follow up."

As Ron shut the door, Nancy propped her feet up on the ottoman. "Sarah – getting back to your question about how pornography harms people – probably one of the main ways it harms people is due to how powerful it is. As I said, sex is a powerful thing God created to bind two people together. Because of this, pornography is able to capture the hearts of many men and women. It does this because of two things you just said – people are born as sexual beings and people are sinful. When people start to view pornography, it creates very powerful urges in their hearts and minds."

"I understand that it's powerful," said Sarah, "but, what do you mean that it captures their hearts?"

"Well, the Bible talks about people becoming enslaved to sin when they give themselves over to a particular sin. This is part of the reason why the Bible tells us to 'flee sexual immorality.' Not only is the Bible telling us to do that, because our body doesn't belong to us and because the Holy Spirit lives inside of us, it is also telling us to flee sexual immorality because it possesses a power. The more one indulges in sexual sin – in this case, pornography – the more they will desire to see pornography. It will create powerful urges in their hearts and those urges will be hard to resist."

"Wow. That's scary."

"Yes, it is, Sarah. And, there's more to that. God is an amazing Creator and he actually created our brains to release certain chemicals when men and women have sex.[2] One chemical is called 'dopamine.' Have you ever heard of that?" Sarah shook her head.

"Dopamine is a chemical that's released in the brain when someone views pornography. This chemical makes our brain desire more and more pornography. What happens, over time, is that the brain releases less dopamine, so people have to look at more pornography to get the same feeling they once had. This is why many people, including myself, believe that pornography is addictive. Do you know what that means?"

"Well, I know you've talked about being addicted to coffee."

With a big smile, Nancy said, "That's right, I have said that. While drinking coffee isn't necessarily sinful, I have to drink it every day or I'd have a headache. Part of the reason for this is an addiction, which means I feel like I have to have it every day. Well, it's similar with pornography. Some people look at it so much, they feel like they have to have it every day. Like I said, it's a powerful thing. Again, this is why God gives us rules with his gift of sex. He does it to protect us because he knows we'll end up hurting ourselves if we misuse his gift."

"I understand," said Sarah. "God is a loving Father and he puts boundaries in place to protect us."

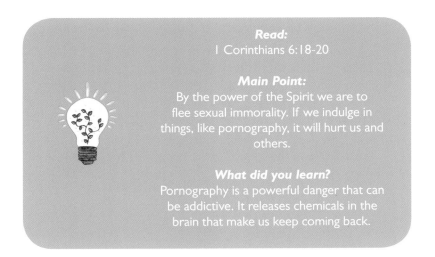

Read:
I Corinthians 6:18-20

Main Point:
By the power of the Spirit we are to flee sexual immorality. If we indulge in things, like pornography, it will hurt us and others.

What did you learn?
Pornography is a powerful danger that can be addictive. It releases chemicals in the brain that make us keep coming back.

2. See endnotes

8. The Gift's Purpose

Read:
Ephesians 5:31-32

Main Point:
Sex is created for marriage and marriage illustrates God's love for his church.

What did you learn?
God's design of sex and marriage ultimately point us to his love for his church. Jesus Christ's finished work keeps us securely in the Father's love and he is ready to forgive sexual sin and give us the power to fight against it.

"There's so much more I need to tell you about this important topic, but we need to get ready for dinner. So let me tell you one last important truth."

"Okay," said Sarah.

"Do you remember what the context for sex is?"

Nodding, Sarah said, "Marriage."

"That's right. That's very important. You see, the Bible tells us that marriage is an earthly picture of God's love for his church. Marriage is supposed to be an unbreakable bond between one man and one woman. Sadly, that's not always the case in our broken world, but that's how God created it. And, it's through this unbreakable bond, that God is saying that he will always love his people and nothing can ever break that. Do you know why that bond can never be broken?"

"Is it because of Jesus?"

"Exactly! Jesus lived a sinless, perfect life and gives that righteousness to his children, by faith. But, what else did he do?"

"He took our sin on him when he died on the cross."

"That's correct! Someone had to pay for our sin and God had to punish in order to be just. So, Jesus perfectly clothed us in righteousness and paid for the punishment our sin deserved. Now, do you know what the Bible calls the people of God?"

"Um, haven't you told me that the church is called the Bride of Christ?"

"Right again, we are God's Bride and this gets us back to marriage. God's design of sex was to take place in marriage. When God told Adam and Eve to enjoy sex in the context of marriage, part of his purpose was to get us to see his love for his church. God is committed to always loving his people and his love is so steadfast, he sent his Son to save us."

"So, what does all of this have to do with pornography?" said Sarah.

"Well, sexual immorality and pornography distort the picture of God's love for his Bride. This is why sexual sin is such a big deal. It's taking something God has a great purpose for and abuses it. Sexual sin is something you are going to be tempted with. Pornography is something you are going to be bombarded with. Sadly, you will see it again, but I hope this talk has helped prepare you for pornography when you see it again."

"Oh, I know it has."

"Lastly, when you do see pornography again or when you lust, remember Jesus paid for those sins too. You professed faith in him last year. Remember he has covered you with his righteousness and paid the penalty of your sin. He gave you the Holy Spirit. Pray for strength from the Spirit to fight against sexual sin and live out God's love as his child."

"Yes Ma'am. Thanks for talking with me Mom. Love you."

"Love you, too."

Conclusion

Pornography is a sad reality of this world we live in. It is something that has ruined individuals, families, marriages, ministries and churches. Even though some people claim it is simply a part of growing up, it is a horrific evil Christians must fight against. It is my hope and prayer that this little workbook could assist individuals, families, marriages, ministries and churches in that fight.

Even though pornography wounds many and leaves those in a wake of destruction, we must not lose heart because we have One who was wounded in order to bring redemption. Pornography is no match for the finished work of Jesus Christ.

If you are one who has looked at pornography or continues to look at pornography, Jesus offers forgiveness. If you are one who gets discouraged in your fight against pornography, the Spirit gives you strength. If you are a parent who is terrified for your child growing up in a world filled with pornography, know that your Heavenly Father loves you as his child and will graciously guide your family through this dark world.

Remember, there is a day coming when pornography will not exist. Jesus lived, died, rose and ascended and he's coming back. He's coming back to make all things new and take his Bride home … forever.

Not If, But When

The Boy's Story

1. One of God's Greatest Gifts

"How was the waterpark?" Hardie asked. Samuel and several of his friends had been anticipating the trip for the past month as it marked the end of school.

"It was such fun, Dad!" Samuel replied. "All my friends were there and it didn't rain like we thought it would. Plus, there was no school."

Laughing, his father said, "I'm glad you had fun, but remember, school isn't something adults do to punish children. It helps you steward the brain God has given you." This was a phrase that had become very familiar to Samuel.

"Hey Dad," Samuel said somberly. "You know how you said we can talk to you about anything?"

"Yes, of course." Hardie, sensed concern in Samuel's tone.

"Well, a couple of my friends saw a girl at the waterpark. She was in a bikini. They talked about how hot she was. Then they said something about sex."

"Thanks so much for telling me this," said Hardie. "Sadly, a lot of guys are going to talk like this and that doesn't honor women in a way God calls us to. Do you remember exactly what they said about sex?"

"Nothing much. They just used the word. I don't even think they knew what it meant."

"Listen, I'm so glad you're coming to me with this and not to someone else. You're showing a lot of wisdom to talk with someone older about something as important as sex. To be honest, I should have talked to you about this sooner, so please forgive me for not doing that. Do you remember how the Bible begins?"

"Yes," said Samuel. "It tells us that God made all things; that he created men and women 'after his own image.'"

"That's right," said Hardie. "And, God also tells humans to be 'fruitful and multiply' and 'to fill the earth.' What do you think God's talking about there?"

Samuel, scratching his head, replied, "Is God telling them to make babies?"

Hardie said, "That is part of what he's telling them. You see, when we read Genesis we read that God made everything. But, it doesn't specifically say that God created sex. Even though it doesn't use the word 'sex' that is some of what is meant by 'fill the earth and multiply.' God wants men and women to have sex in the proper context."

Samuel thought about what his dad said, "So, sex is how babies are made?"

"That's right," said Hardie. "You know how Mom and Dad tell you that you are an amazing gift to us? Well, sex is also an amazing gift. God made it and gave it to us and it is just one of the many ways that tells us what a gracious and loving God we have."

Samuel replied, "So when sex is a good thing why did I feel like we were talking about something bad when my friends brought it up at the waterpark?"

"That's a great question, son. Let's go on the back deck and talk about this some more."

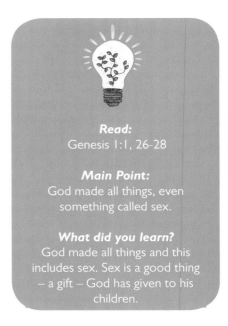

Read:
Genesis 1:1, 26-28

Main Point:
God made all things, even something called sex.

What did you learn?
God made all things and this includes sex. Sex is a good thing – a gift – God has given to his children.

2. The Gift's Instructions

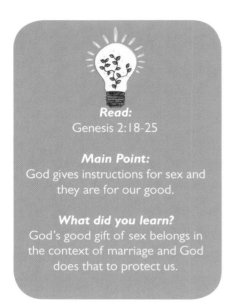

Read:
Genesis 2:18-25

Main Point:
God gives instructions for sex and they are for our good.

What did you learn?
God's good gift of sex belongs in the context of marriage and God does that to protect us.

As Hardie poured a lemonade, Samuel finished his in one enormous gulp.

"Slow down and enjoy it," Hardie laughed.

"I'm thirsty! It was so hot at the waterpark."

"Samuel, you asked an insightful question about sex. You said that you felt guilty when you talked about it?"

"Yes."

"Well, there's a few reasons why you felt that way. The first thing you should know about sex is that it is an intimate action between a husband and wife. Genesis 2 says, 'the man and his wife were both naked and were not ashamed.' They were not ashamed because sin had not entered the earth. There was no shame in them being naked because it was just the two of them. I know they were the only two people on the earth, but sex is a very private and intimate thing. Something that's just supposed to be shared between a husband and wife. It's not something your friends should talk about at the waterpark. Especially since they probably don't even know what it means."

"That makes sense," said Samuel. "But if it's a good thing God made and it's a gift he's given to us, why is it so secret and why did I feel guilty?"

Pouring another glass of lemonade, Hardie said, "Well, since God created sex, he also gives us instructions on how humans should enjoy this good gift. And, just like the gift God gives, the instructions are good too. They are there to protect us. And, two important instructions God gives about sex have to do with context and timing."

"Context and timing?" Samuel questioned. "What exactly do you mean?"

Thinking intently, Hardie said, "Samuel, do you remember that time you got in trouble with Mrs. Smith?"

Feeling a sense of shame, Samuel said, "Yes."

Hardie quickly replied, "Listen, I'm not trying to make you feel guilty. We talked about it and you are forgiven. I just want to explain context to you. You see, Mrs. Smith punished you and your friends because you were talking in class. But, is talking with your friends a bad thing?"

A bit unsure, Samuel replied, "No?"

"Well," said Hardie, "you could say 'yes.' There are times you can talk and times you can't. Talking while the teacher is speaking is one time when you can't. There are contexts when you can talk with friends and contexts when you can't."

"That makes sense," said Samuel. "So, there are times when you can have sex and times when you can't."

"Exactly!" said Hardie. "The Bible tells us that sex is only okay in the context of marriage. Whenever you take God's good gift of sex out of his good instructions on context, it actually ends up hurting us. Does that make sense?"

Nodding, Samuel replied, "Yes, I understand. That's why I felt a little guilty talking about it with my friends."

Hardie nodded, "Now, let me explain what I mean by timing …"

3. Opening the Gift too Early

Hardie's focus was diverted to the sound of the backdoor swinging open as he saw Duke – the family dog – being chased by his daughter, Sarah.

"Sorry to interrupt! I was trying to give Duke a bath, but …"

"Oh, we know how that goes," said Hardie. "He loves to get muddy, but he doesn't like to get clean. Listen" said Hardie. "I'm having a talk with Samuel that I had with you a couple of years ago."

"Oh…' the talk,'" said Sarah, smiling.

"That's right," said Hardie. "I know we still talk about this, but let me just talk to Samuel right now."

"I completely understand," said Sarah.

"Now where were we?" said Hardie.

"Marriage is the context for sex," Samuel said. "You were about to say something about timing?"

"That's right! Good memory, son. There's a verse that's repeated in the biblical book called the Song of Solomon. It's a book about love and marriage. One verse that's repeated many times is this, 'Do not stir up or awaken love until it pleases.' A basic understanding of this verse means that there's also an appropriate time for sex."

Samuel kicked his feet up on the table as he listened to his father. "You see, since God created man and woman for sex, we are sexual beings. What that means is we all have sexual desires in us. Your friends, for example, at the waterpark were expressing some sexual desires when they saw that girl. How would you apply the verse from the Song of Solomon to this situation with your friends?"

A bit surprised by the question, Samuel said, "Uh … I guess … it would mean that we should be careful talking about girls? I mean, we could be stirring up desires too soon?"

"That's a really thoughtful answer. You are right. You have to be careful talking about sex and love because they are strong desires that God has created. He has created them to bind two people together in a deep way. So, if you talk about sexual desires too often, you might 'awaken love' in a way that's removing it from its proper context."

"Dad, if talking about sexual desires might awaken love too soon, is it bad for us to be talking about it? I mean, I'm thinking about it right now, so is this a bad thing?"

"That's such a smart question," said Hardie. "As your dad, it's part of my job to tell you about sex and love. Remember, God has created you as a sexual being, so you're going to have sexual desires regardless of whether or not your mother and I talk about it. You see, we need to have these talks, so you know what to do when you have these desires. You don't need to feel guilty for having these desires, because God gave them to you. One thing you need to do when you feel those desires is that you talk to me or Mom and, most importantly, talk to God about them in prayer."

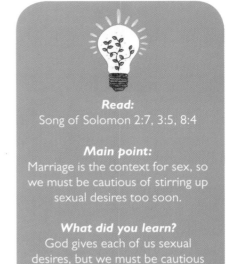

Read:
Song of Solomon 2:7, 3:5, 8:4

Main point:
Marriage is the context for sex, so we must be cautious of stirring up sexual desires too soon.

What did you learn?
God gives each of us sexual desires, but we must be cautious of stirring those emotions up too soon.

4. Distorting the Gift

"Hey Dad." As those words came out of Samuel's mouth, Hardie sensed a tone of guilt. "Something else happened at the waterpark. When we were finishing up for the day, Danny showed me some pictures he had on his phone. They were pictures of girls and a few of them were naked."

"I am so sorry you saw that."

"You told me I could talk to you about anything, so I wanted to tell you about this."

Hardie leaned forward and patted Samuel on the knee. "I'm so happy you told me. You did the right thing. Samuel, those pictures are something we call pornography. Pornography is pictures of people that are either naked or barely clothed."

"Dad, I knew I shouldn't be looking at them and I didn't look at them long, but I was caught off guard when Danny showed them too me. I felt like it would be weird if I didn't look or he'd make fun of me if I told him to put the phone down. I didn't know what to do, so I just acted like I liked them, but there was part of me that did like them."

"I completely understand," said Hardie. "This is part of why it is so important for us to talk about sex. Sadly, we live in a sinful world and humans have taken God's good gift of sex and distorted it in many ways. Pornography is just one way sinful humans distort the gift of sex."

"Dad, why are my friends looking at pornography?"

Hardie paused to think a minute before he responded. "Well, if you think about what we've discussed, it makes sense. God created all of us to be sexual creatures, but those desires are to occur in the proper context. Pornography steals parts of God's gift and uses it in inappropriate and evil ways. So, in other words, your friends are enticed by pornography – in part – because they're created as sexual beings and this is part of the reason you also liked what you saw. Does that make sense?"

"I think it does."

Hardie explained it once more, "Even though pornography is taking sexual desires out of their context, it still contains aspects of God's good gift of sex."

"I get it," said Samuel.

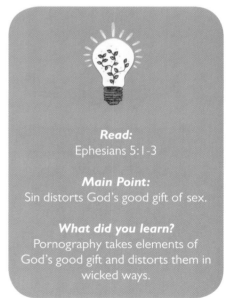

Read:
Ephesians 5:1-3

Main Point:
Sin distorts God's good gift of sex.

What did you learn?
Pornography takes elements of God's good gift and distorts them in wicked ways.

"And that's what makes pornography so dangerous. It is using elements of God's gift, but it's twisting them in horrible ways. This is what Paul meant when he talked about sexual immorality. There are a lot of things that could be described as sexual immorality, pornography is one of them."

5. Worshiping the Gift

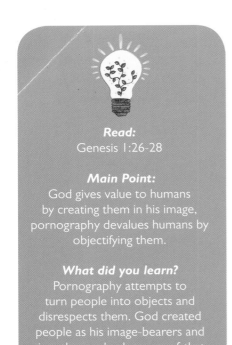

Read:
Genesis 1:26-28

Main Point:
God gives value to humans by creating them in his image, pornography devalues humans by objectifying them.

What did you learn?
Pornography attempts to turn people into objects and disrespects them. God created people as his image-bearers and gives them value because of that.

Hardie could tell that Samuel was pretty upset by what he had seen. He moved over near his son and patted his back. "Son, I know this was an upsetting thing for you and I'm so sorry you had to see those pictures. Part of the reason you are so upset is because of how God created us as humans. You see, he has created everyone – male and female, young and old, black or white – 'after his own image.' Therefore, every human reflects his glory and deserves respect. Pornography, however, disrespects people."

"Dad, I know pornography is wrong by removing sex out of the context you talked about, but how does it disrespect people?"

"I don't want to upset you, but I want to ask you a question about that picture you saw. Do you remember the girl's face in the picture?" asked Hardie.

"It didn't show her face, Dad."

"That's what I thought. Often pornography doesn't focus on the faces of the men or women in the pictures. Sometimes it does, but sometimes it doesn't. What pornography does is focus on body parts. In a sense, it's trying to just give us pictures of the sexual parts of people, without us seeing the person. The word for this is 'objectifying.' Pornography tells us to focus on people as objects for us to use how we want, instead of seeing them as people. This goes against the way God created us."

"I understand. God made all of us to reflect his image," said Samuel, "but pornography tries to get us to focus on different parts of people, which … objectifies them and disrespects them?"

"That's right. Once again, it's taking sex out of the context God created it for. It's taking sex out of the context of marriage and tries to give it to people in a way that's inappropriate. Pornography tricks people into thinking they can take God's gift and use it in another way, but they only end up hurting themselves when they do that. Remember, sex was created to bind a man and a woman together in a loving way. Pornography removes the loving relationship of our sexuality and focuses on sexual parts."

"Now that I think about it," said Samuel, "when Danny was showing us the pictures he had on his phone, all of the other guys around were just talking about the body parts. They weren't talking about that girl as a person."

"Yes, and this goes against the way God created humans. Again, people are God's image-bearers and that means they deserve respect, but pornography attempts to take that away from people. Pornography disrespects people."

"I see. I felt bad after seeing those pictures and I see how pornography disrespects people … but, why did my friends enjoy it?"

"That's an important question," said Hardie.

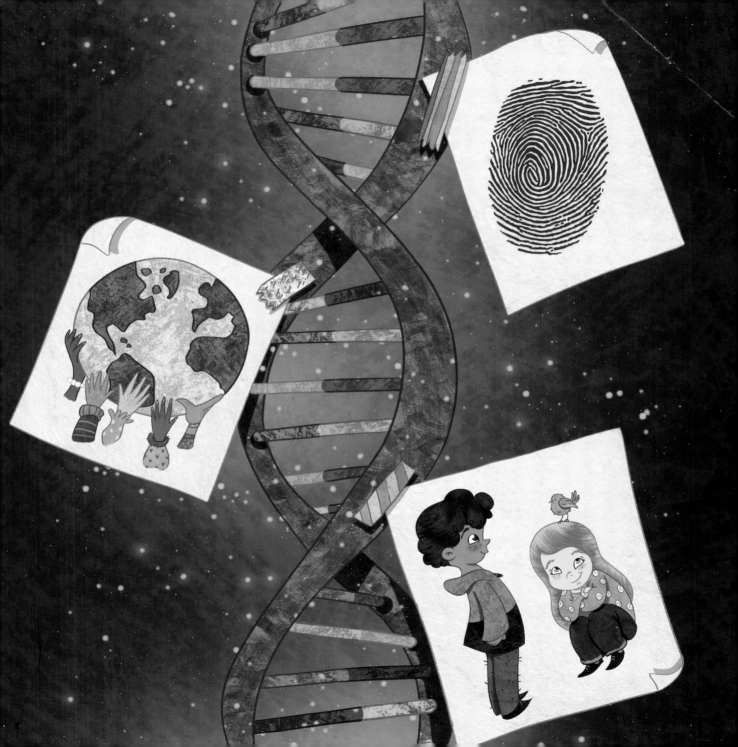

6. Enjoying the Gift

Read:
Matthew 5:27-30

"As I told you earlier, God created every person with sexual desires[1]. But, every human on the face of the earth is also a sinner; therefore, these sexual desires can get confused. To say it another way, the good sexual desires God gave us can also become sinful."

"So, my friends were looking at those pictures, because God created them as sexual people?"

"That's right."

"But, they were in sin, because they weren't using the desires in a way God created them to?"

"Exactly," said Hardie. "We often refer to sexual sin as lust. Lust can refer to more than our sexuality, but it means a really strong desire for something you cannot have. When Jesus was speaking in the Sermon on the Mount, he warned us about lust. You see, many people in his day thought they were obeying the Ten Commandments because they didn't literally commit adultery with another person's spouse. But, Jesus teaches that if you even lust after someone in your heart you are committing adultery with them in your mind."

Main Point:
God gives humans sexual desires, but sin often turns that into lust.

What did you learn?
God gives all of us sexual desires that are good. Because of our sin, they affect those desires and we can sin against God by lusting.

"Were my friends lusting when they looked at those pictures?"

"Most likely they were."

"Was I lusting, Dad?"

"Well, it sounds like you were upset because you were caught off guard by these images. You also were not seeking them out, so in a sense, you weren't lusting after these images. That said, the images were sinful and inappropriate for you to look at. The important thing is that you told me about them and now we're able to have this talk."

"I understand."

"Son, you don't need to feel bad that you will have sexual desires in your life. Remember, God created you to have sexual attraction. Does that make sense?" Samuel nodded in agreement.

"The important truth is that you ask the Holy Spirit to help you with those desires. When Jesus taught about lusting, he was telling everyone how badly they need him. When he spoke on lusting, he was telling everyone that they sin sexually and need him to cleanse them. Samuel, you will not be able to live a perfect life, especially when it comes to sex, but you can ask God to give you strength to honor him with your sexuality. Let's pray and ask God for that now."

1. See endnotes

48

...m, his dad could tell he was processing the conversation. Instead of speaking, Hardie just sat in ...ink.

...e the silence and said, "I know I've got a question; but let me think back through all you've said."
...ded.

"God created men and women and invented sex as a good thing," said Samuel.

Hardie nodded in affirmation.

"He made us as sexual beings in his image, but we sinned against him."

Nodding again, Hardie said, "That's correct."

"Pornography is a result of our sin and it objectifies people and causes us to lust … which is like adultery."

"All of that is correct, son."

"Are there other ways that pornography hurts people?"

"Yes, there are. Actually, there are many, many ways it hurts people."

The discussion was interrupted with a knock at the door. Hardie's wife, Helen, entered the room and could tell the two were engaged in a serious discussion. "Were you still planning on grilling burgers tonight?"

"Yes. I can get on that in just a little bit. Samuel and I are talking about sex and pornography."

"No rush! That's an important conversation," said Helen. "Just let me know if you need me to help with anything."

As Helen shut the door, Hardie propped his feet up on the ottoman. "Samuel – getting back to your question about how pornography harms people – one of the main ways it harms people is due to how powerful it is. As I said, sex is a powerful thing God created to bind two people together. Because of this, pornography is able to capture the hearts of many men and women. It does this because of two things you just said – people are born as sexual beings and people are sinful. When people start to view pornography it creates very powerful urges in their hearts and minds."

"I understand that it's powerful," said Samuel, "but, what do you mean that it captures their hearts?"

"Well, the Bible talks about people becoming enslaved to sin when they give themselves over to a particular sin. This is part of the reason why the Bible tells us to 'flee sexual immorality.' Not only is the Bible telling us to do that, because our body doesn't belong to us and because the Holy Spirit lives inside of us, it is also telling us to flee sexual immorality because it possesses a power. The more one indulges in sexual sin – in this case, pornography – the more they will desire to see pornography. It will create powerful urges in their hearts and those urges will be hard to resist."

"Wow. That's scary."

"Yes, it is, Samuel. And, there's more to that. God is an amazing Creator and he actually created our brains to release certain chemicals when men and women have sex.[2] One chemical is called 'dopamine.' Have you ever heard of that?" Samuel shook his head.

"Dopamine is a chemical that's released in the brain when someone views pornography. This chemical makes our brain desire more and more pornography. What happens, over time, is that the brain releases less dopamine, so people have to look at more pornography to get the same feeling they once had. This is why many people, including myself, believe that pornography is addictive. Do you know what that means?"

"Well, I know you've talked about being addicted to coffee."

With a big smile, Hardie said, "That's right, I have said that. While drinking coffee isn't necessarily sinful, I have to drink it every day or I'd have a headache. Part of the reason for this is an addiction, which means I feel like I have to have it every day. Well, it's similar with pornography. Some people look at it so much, they feel like they have to have it every day. Like I said, it's a powerful thing. Again, this is why God gives us rules with his gift of sex. He does it to protect us because he knows we'll end up hurting ourselves if we misuse his gift."

"I understand," said Samuel. "God is a loving Father and he puts boundaries in place to protect us."

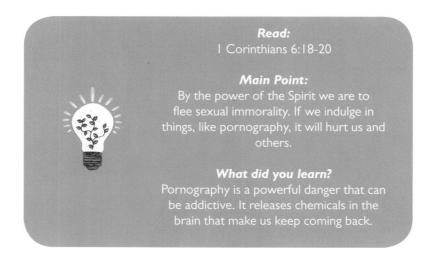

Read:
1 Corinthians 6:18-20

Main Point:
By the power of the Spirit we are to flee sexual immorality. If we indulge in things, like pornography, it will hurt us and others.

What did you learn?
Pornography is a powerful danger that can be addictive. It releases chemicals in the brain that make us keep coming back.

2. See endnotes

8. The Gift's Purpose

"Samuel, there's more I need to tell you about this very important topic, but we need to get ready for dinner. So, let me tell you one last important truth. Do you remember what the context for sex is?"

Nodding, Samuel said, "Marriage."

"That's right. That's very important. You see, the Bible tells us that marriage is an earthly picture of God's love for his church. Marriage is supposed to be an unbreakable bond between one man and one woman. Sadly, that's not always the case in our broken world, but that's how God created it. God is saying that he will always love his people and nothing can ever break that. Do you know why that bond can never be broken?"

"Is it because of Jesus?"

"Exactly! Jesus lived a sinless, perfect life and gives that righteousness to his children, by faith. But, what else did he do?"

"He took our sin on him when he died on the cross."

"That's correct! Someone had to pay for our sin and God had to punish in order to be just. So, Jesus perfectly clothed us in righteousness and paid for the punishment our sin deserved. Now, do you know what the Bible calls the people of God?"

"Um, haven't you told me that the church is called the Bride of Christ?"

"Right again, we are God's Bride and this gets us back to marriage. God's design of sex was to take place in marriage. When God told Adam and Eve to enjoy sex in the context of marriage, part of his purpose was to get us to see his love for his church. God is committed to always loving his people and his love is so steadfast, he sent his Son to save us."

"So, what does all of this have to do with pornography?" said Samuel.

"Well, sexual immorality and pornography distort the picture of God's love for his Bride. This is why sexual sin is such a big deal. It's taking something God has a great purpose for and abuses it. Samuel, sexual sin is something you are going to be tempted with. Pornography is something you are going to be bombarded with. Sadly, you will see it again, but I hope this talk has helped prepare you for pornography when you see it again."

"Oh, I know it has."

"Lastly, when you do see pornography again or when you lust, remember that Jesus paid for those sins too. You professed faith in him so remember that he has covered you with his righteousness and paid the penalty of that sin. He also gave you the Holy Spirit. Pray for strength from the Spirit to fight against sexual sin and live out of God's love and acceptance of you as his child."

"I will. Thanks for talking with me Dad. Love you."

"Love you, too."

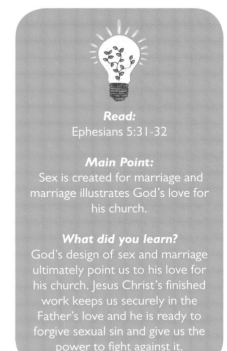

Read:
Ephesians 5:31-32

Main Point:
Sex is created for marriage and marriage illustrates God's love for his church.

What did you learn?
God's design of sex and marriage ultimately point us to his love for his church. Jesus Christ's finished work keeps us securely in the Father's love and he is ready to forgive sexual sin and give us the power to fight against it.

Conclusion

Pornography is a sad reality of this world we live in. It is something that has ruined individuals, families, marriages, ministries and churches. Even though some people claim it is simply a part of growing up, it is a horrific evil Christians must fight against. It is my hope and prayer that this little workbook could assist individuals, families, marriages, ministries and churches in that fight.

Even though pornography wounds many and leaves those in a wake of destruction, we must not lose heart because we have One who was wounded in order to bring redemption. Pornography is no match for the finished work of Jesus Christ.

If you are one who has looked at pornography or continues to look at pornography, Jesus offers forgiveness. If you are one who gets discouraged in your fight against pornography, the Spirit gives you strength. If you are a parent who is terrified for your child growing up in a world filled with pornography, know that your Heavenly Father loves you as his child and will graciously guide your family through this dark world.

Remember, there is a day coming when pornography will not exist. Jesus lived, died, rose and ascended and he's coming back. He's coming back to make all things new and take his Bride home … forever.

1 Page 26, 48 - See Chapter 3

2 Page 31, 52 - The main chemicals are called oxytocin and vasopressin. For more information on this, I would encourage you to read, *Love Thy Body: Answering Hard Questions about Life and Sexuality* by: Nancy Pearcey. Specifically pgs. 127 & 128

10 9 8 7 6 5 4 3 2 1
Copyright © 2020 John Perritt
ISBN: 978-1-5271-0342-9
Published by Christian Focus Publications,
Geanies House, Fearn, Tain, Ross-shire, IV20 1TW, U.K.
Illustrations, Cover and chapter page design by Alice Mastropaolo
Printed in Ukraine

All rights reserved. No part of this publication may be reproduced, stored in a retrieval system, or transmitted, in any form, by any means, electronic, mechanical, photocopying, recording or otherwise without the prior permission of the publisher or a licence permitting restricted copying. In the U.K. such licences are issued by the Copyright Licensing Agency, Saffron House, 6-10 Kirby Street, London, EC1 8TS. www.cla.co.uk

Scripture quotations are from The Holy Bible, English Standard Version, copyright © 2001 by Crossway Bibles, a publishing ministry of Good News Publishers. Used by permission. All rights reserved. ESV Text Edition: 2011.

Reformed Youth Ministries

Reformed Youth Ministries (RYM) exists to reach students for Christ and equip them to serve. Passing the faith on to the next generation has been RYM's passion since it began. In 1972 three youth workers who shared a passion for biblical teaching to youth surveyed the landscape of youth ministry conferences. What they found was an emphasis on fun and games, not God's Word. Therefore, they started a conference that focused on the preaching and teaching of God's Word. Over the years RYM has grown beyond conferences into three areas of ministry: conferences, training, and resources.

Conferences: RYM's youth conferences take place in the summer at a variety of locations across the United States and are continuing to expand. We also host parenting conferences throughout the year at local churches.

Training: RYM launched an annual Youth Leader Training (YLT) conference in 2008. YLT has grown steadily through the years and is offered in multiple locations. RYM also offers a Church Internship Program in partnering local churches as well as youth leader coaching and youth ministry consulting.

Resources: RYM offers a variety of resources for leaders, parents, and students. Several Bible studies are offered as free downloads with more titles regularly being added to their catalogue. RYM hosts multiple podcasts: Parenting Today, The Local Youth Worker, & The RYM Student Podcast – all of which can be downloaded on multiple formats. There are many additional ministry tools available for download on the website.

If you are passionate for passing the faith on to the next generation, please visit www.rym.org to learn more about Reformed Youth Ministries. If you are interested in partnering with us in ministry, please visit www.rym.org/donate.

www.rym.org

Christian Focus Publications

Christian Focus Publications publishes books for adults and children under its four main imprints:
Christian Focus, CF4K, Mentor and Christian Heritage.
Our books reflect our conviction that God's Word is reliable and Jesus is the way to know him, and live for ever with him.

Our children's list includes a Sunday School curriculum that covers pre-school to early teens,
and puzzle and activity books. We also publish personal and family devotional titles,
biographies and inspirational stories that children will love. If you are looking for quality
Bible teaching for children, then we have an excellent range
of Bible stories and age-specific theological books. From pre-school board books to teenage apologetics,
we have it covered!

CF4•K
Because you're never
too young to know Jesus

CHRISTIAN FOCUS PUBLICATIONS
Christian Focus | Christian Heritage | CF4K | Mentor